William Bolcom

Ballade

for Piano

ISBN 978-1-4234-7546-0

EDWARD B. Marks music COMPANY

EXCLUSIVELY DISTRIBUTED BY
HAL•LEONARD® CORPORATION
7777 W. BLUEMOUND RD. P.O. BOX 13819 MILWAUKEE, WI 53213

www.ebmarks.com
www.halleonard.com

commissioned by Ursula Oppens
in memory of Jacqueline Hoefer

Ballade
for Piano

WILLIAM BOLCOM
2006

4

* Match dynamic of overtones.

* Ossia: R.H. coll'8↑ through m. 162, last ♪ (i.e. bottom two C♯'s of keyboard); see p. 3.

14

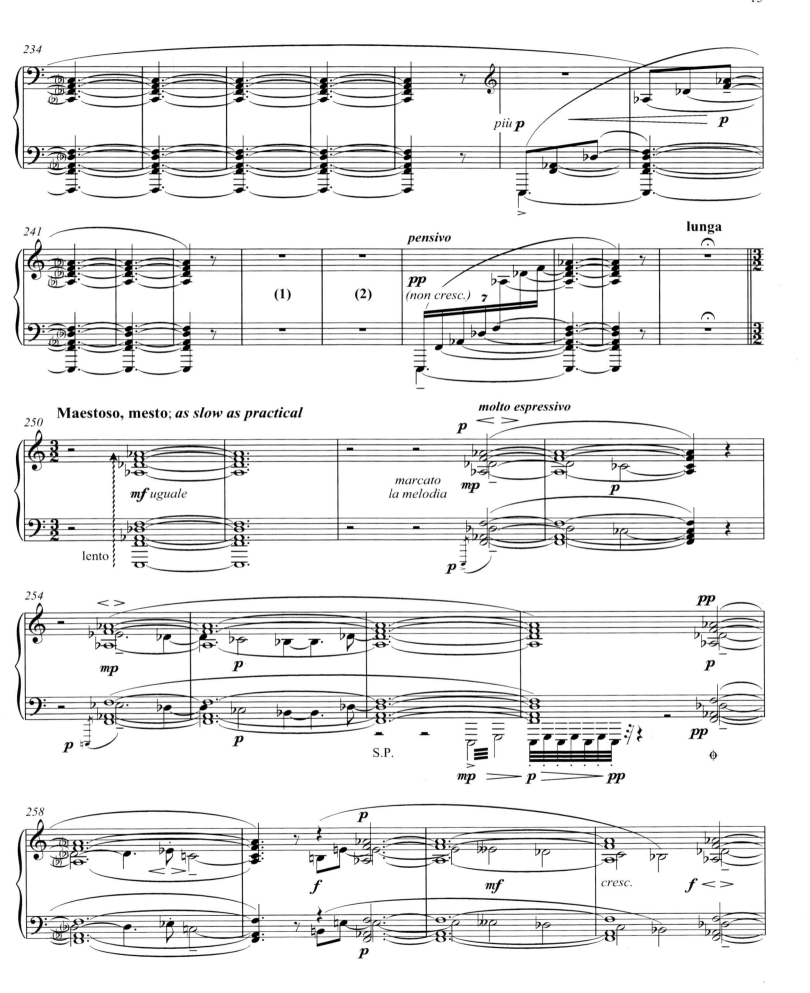

16

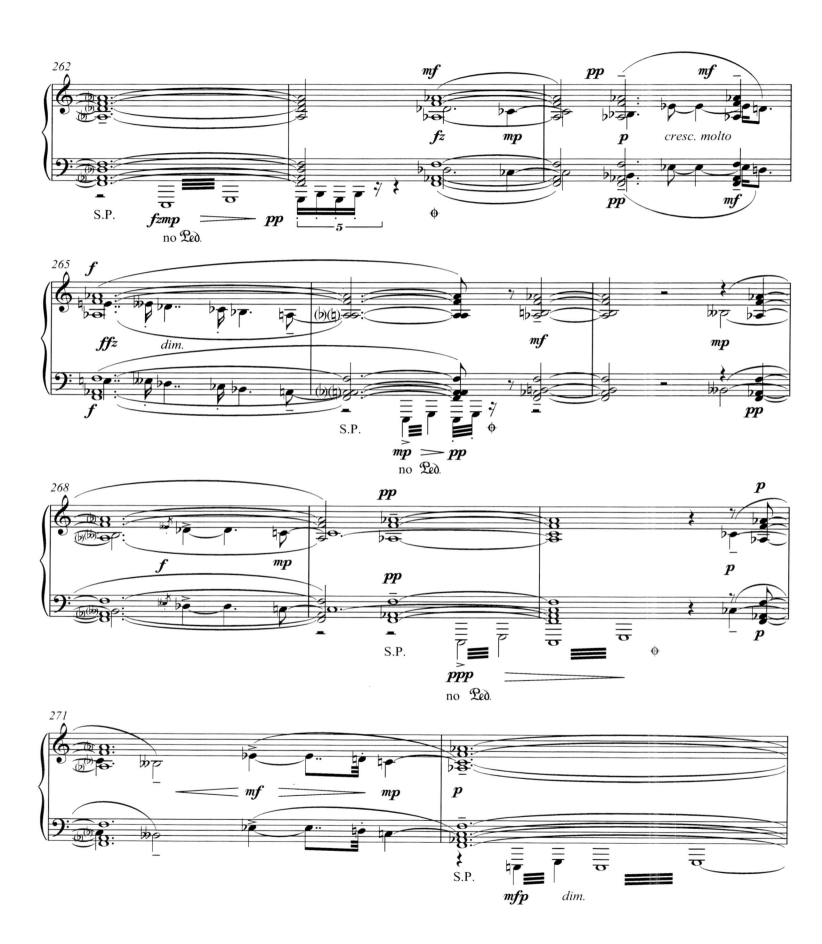

Dec. 30, 2006
Ann Arbor